How to Transform a Small Business

Into a Multimillion Dollar Enterprise

Colvin Tonya Nyakundi

Business and Entrepreneurial Series

JD-Biz Publishing

Check out some of the other Entrepreneur Series books

Entrepreneur Series books on Amazon

Table of Contents

Introduction

Tens of thousands of small businesses are registered in the United States each year but not all of them survive for even one year. Whereas there are those that thrive and make huge profits within a few months, others collapse within a very short period of time. There are also those that stagnate i.e. they make some profit but their profits never grow and their clientele remains constant for a number of years.

All those interested in opening a business should learn how to grow their small businesses into multimillion dollar enterprises. Without practical ideas on how to transform a business, an investor can end up being one of the many examples of failed ventures. Regardless of the number of years you've been doing business, a simple mistake can make your business change from one of the most profitable ventures into a loss making entity.

A business that performs quite well in a given market/environment could make loses in another market due to the variance in choices and preferences in different parts of the world. This means that potential entrepreneurs must come up with ideas on how to grow their businesses in a particular market.

Running a business involves several risks and uncertainties as market conditions are dynamic and can change rapidly without warning or clear indicators. This means that entrepreneurs must always be prepared to adopt contingency plans once the market conditions become unfavorable for given types of business. If you're keen on transforming your business into a dominant player in your industry you must have some clues on what to do when the market isn't favoring you.

This book is designed to help all those planning to start a small business and grow it into a multimillion dollar venture with consistent profits. With this book, you can rest assured that your business will grow as it contains tips on what to do and what not to do when it comes to business ventures. No need to worry about the nature of business because the book can be used in all types of businesses including service delivery, manufacturing, hospitality sector, distribution, marketing and retailing.

"How to Transform a Small Business into a Multimillion Dollar Enterprise" also contains ideas about what businessmen and women should do during a recession or harsh economic conditions.

Grow your business into a recognizable and profitable entity by simply reading this book up to the end!!!

Overcoming challenges facing Small Businesses

Newly established businesses encounter numerous challenges during the first few months or years of their existence. The way in which an entrepreneur handles this challenges is the greatest determinant on whether the business is going to be successful or not. If the entrepreneur deals with this challenges perfectly, then he/she can rest assured that the business will grow in customer numbers and profits and probably become one of the dominant players in that industry/market. On the other hand if he/she fails to tackle these issues flawlessly, there is a very high likelihood that the business will collapse within a very short period of time.

Here are some of the challenges facing small newly established businesses and practical tips on how to avoid or counter them:

- Inadequate resources to pay employees and continue production before profits start trickling in.

Take a look into the history of some of the largest corporations in the world and you'll discover that most of them have one thing in common; they faced serious financial problems during the first few years of their existence. The fact that they survived this challenge and are now making massive profits is an indication that they handled it properly. If you recently registered a business but you don't have the money to run it for a few more weeks or months, going for a bank loan could be your way out of that predicament. Another way of raising the necessary funds is by listing the business/company on the securities/stock exchange. You can also decide to partner with other companies and individuals willing to buy shares in the company. If all the above sources of income are just not working, then you can decide to dispose of some of the company assets that you deem not very important. Remember that you can reacquire the assets once the business starts making profits.

- Low sales and unsustainable customer numbers

Once you start a business you can find yourself in a situation where you have overstocked products and the warehouse is almost full but there is nobody to buy the merchandise. If you are offering services, the number of people seeking them could be unsustainable while you still need to pay your employees, pay for utility services and office space. What do you do now? Well, you can come out of this problem by adopting a vigorous marketing campaign inviting potential customers to come and experience your products and/or services. Effective marketing strategies are addressed in another part of this book so keep on reading. You can also reduce the amount you're charging so as to increase sales even thorough the profit made on each item is reduced. Keep in mind that your main aim is to attract as many customers as possible. If you're offering services, you can decide to reduce the amount you charge clients per session. Before effecting any price changes, it is important that you consider your competitors so as to adopt prices that encourage potential clients to leave their regular service providers and try yours.

- Trademark development, company logo and slogan

When you see an IPhone® or Windows® computer, you don't need anybody to tell you that this is an 'Apple Inc®" or "Microsoft Corp®" product. You just look at the companies' logo and immediately recognize their products. It is irrefutable that these two companies are some of the largest in the world as they are even listed on the fortune 500 companies. If you have a deep desire to transform your small business/company into a multimillion dollar enterprise, you must make sure that you have the best logo/trademark and company slogan. Qualities of a good logo include uniqueness, attractiveness and positivity. In the example of Apple or Blackberry phones, the companies adopted sweet and popular fruits that everybody likes. Can you imagine what could have happened if the two companies had decided to name their products negative names such as 'tsunami,' 'storm,' 'tornado' or 'crocodile?' Whichever name you decide to give your business or company you must make sure that it conveys a positive message.

- Logistics of forming a countrywide/worldwide distribution network

Unlike well established companies/businesses, newly established ones don't have a countrywide/worldwide network of distributing their products. These new companies might lack enough trucks, refrigerated vans and distributors in different regions. To counter the challenge of transporting products from the main factory/warehouse to the distributor, you can decide to hire trucks or refrigerated vans for a short period of time before buying yours once you start making significant profits. So as to ensure that you have distributers everywhere you need to give investors reasons as to why they should sell your products. You can do this by giving them incentives such as giving them a high dividend on each sold unit. You can also decide to directly control your distribution network by establishing warehouses in each region you want to sell the products.

- Hiring the most qualified and experienced workers

One of the main challenges facing newly established companies/businesses is lack of skilled and experienced manpower. Maybe the most experienced workers are working for rival companies or they're not willing to work with you. The best way to ensure that you hire and retain the best employees in your industry is by giving them incentives. For instance you can provide free health insurance to your employees and their families as a way of ensuring that they are happy and satisfied working with you. You also have to make sure that they receive reasonable salaries and in a timely manner. When one of the employees is planning to acquire a loan, you can decide to be his/her guarantor as a way of encouraging them to continue working with you. Giving allowances such as house allowance, holiday allowance, commuting allowance and free education for their children is also one of the ways in which you can hire and retain the best employees. The conditions under which your employees are working should also be favorable and not endangering them in any way. If for instance your company is dealing in dangerous chemicals or moving machines, the employees must be provided with protective gear whenever they're working within the company premises.

- Technological advancements as easier cheaper and efficient labor

Most of the large corporations invest millions of dollars each year in research so as to come up with more advanced technology as an easier, cheaper and more efficient source of labor. If you recently opened a company, investing some of the money towards the innovation of more advanced technology is the best way to go. If you don't have the money required for such research, you can purchase the rights to use patented technology from already existing companies.

- Sabotage from well established companies

Even though large companies will never publicly admit to sabotage, they always do it once they feel threatened by small emerging companies. If you're facing this challenge, the best way to handle it is by making sure that your competitors don't have a clue about what you are planning i.e. your marketing tactics, recent innovations and how you plan to run the company. Always make sure that confidential files and company secrets remain secret at all costs. If you have proof of sabotage, you can decide to seek legal redress so that the sabotaging company can be fined or compensate you for damages.

- Negative publicity and slandering

Newly established businesses might occasionally be slandered by their competitors in a deliberate effort to make sure that potential customers perceive the company negatively. You can deal with this challenge by ensuring you provide high quality products and services at all costs and steering clear of any kind of controversy.

- Dealing with unsatisfied clients

Throughout this world, no company has ever been able to satisfy all clients by meeting all their expectations. So as to ensure that your company maintains its good name and reputation you must know how to deal with all those clients who are dissatisfied with the quality or nature of products and services they received. Always make sure that all your clients' concerns are addressed in a timely manner.

If possible, unsatisfied clients can be given back their money and return purchased products.

Establishing a Distinguishable Brand

Imagine starting a company that nobody has ever heard off before, nobody knows their offices or the type of services or products being offering. Even though it looks like a very difficult task, transforming your brand into one of the most distinguishable ones isn't very difficult. With the tips listed below, you can easily and quickly transform a small business into a dominant figure in a particular industry.

- Patenting products

Patenting your products is one of the ways in which you can make sure that your company grows into a distinguishable brand. Once you develop a new product, you must patent it so that your competitors don't offer the same kind of products that you're offering. This way a potential client will have no choice than your brand when they're interested in specific aspects of the product.

- Innovation of new products

After using a given product for some time, consumers may start feeling bored and hence decide to look for alternatives. If you are interested in establishing a distinguishable brand, you have to make sure that your company is the leader in innovation and coming up with new products at least annually. By simply coming up with new, more advanced and easy to use products, your company will become one of the leading brands in that industry. It is also important that you avoid starting a business that deals in outdated technologies or products. One perfect example is the typewriter. In this era, it is totally illogical to start a company that manufactures and/or sells typewriters. Most motor vehicle companies are changing from the manufacture of cars with manual gears to those with automatic gears. If you're thinking of starting such a company, you might want to start one that manufactures automatic cars with more advanced features.

- Provision of many different types of products or services

Due to the fact that most people experience mood swings at different times of the day or year, consumers' choices and preferences are bound to change from time to time. Therefore more and more people will prefer your brand to your competitors' once they're guaranteed of a wide variety of products and services to choose from. If for example you are planning to start a company that processes food, you can decide to sell the packed meals in different flavors so that consumers have a wide variety to choose from. If you are planning to manufacture desktop and/or laptop computers, ensuring that the final products run on different types of operating systems is one way of ensuring that your brand becomes distinguishable within a short period of time.

- Maintaining high quality products or service delivery

Always make sure that your company/business is offering high quality products, service delivery and customer care relations. Once a client is satisfied with what you have to offer, he/she will probably inform their friends, family and colleagues and soon your company will grow into a distinguishable brand. You must also make sure that the consumers are not in any danger by using your products. This means that you must always make sure that you put in place safety measures and warnings meant to protect users of given products. Large auto companies such as Toyota and General Motors have in the past recalled millions of cars due to safety concerns. Even though they spend millions of dollars in recalling such cars, they still make huge profits because most people still trust these companies as they know that the companies are doing everything possible to guarantee their safety.

- Associating your company with other distinguishable companies

Instead of just eating bread, most people prefer eating bread with butter/margarine. However, it is quite difficult to find a company that bakes bread and manufactures butter concurrently. If you are thinking of starting a bakery, you might want to partner with an established company that manufactures butter/margarine. Once your brand is associated with other leading brands offering related products, you can easily transform your company into a distinguishable one within a very short duration. If you're planning to register a publishing company, partnering with reputable print paper and ink manufacturers is one way of making sure that your company is easily recognizable.

- Participating in charitable activities

After your company starts making profits, it is important that you dedicate a given percentage of the profits to a charitable course such as provision of wheelchairs for the poor and disabled, paying medical fees for diabetic and cancer patients, renovating and equipping public health facilities, sponsoring poor but intelligent students to top universities and refurbishing amenities in public schools. Once your business/company is associated with a given charitable event, it will definitely grow into one of the leading brands as more people will prefer your products to your competitors'.

- Do what you do best

You can also significantly grow your company by simply offering services or products that you're experienced in or familiar with. "Kentucky Fried chicken (KFC®)" is one of the most notable brands when it comes to processed chicken. The founder of this fast food chain (Colonel Harland Sanders) started cooking and selling chicken in 1930 and currently there are more than ten thousand outlets worldwide in more than a hundred countries. He decided to start this business simply because he knew he was good at frying chicken and hence he can offer tasty products that meet consumers' expectations. One other good example is "McDonald's Corporation®" which was founded in 1940 in San Bernardino, Ca as a small restaurant but is now the largest food chain in the world. You can also transform your business into a leading brand by simply doing what you do best.

- Avoid boardroom wrangles and court cases

Apart from portraying a company negatively, boardroom wrangles and court cases may derail implementation of important strategies. For a company/business to establish itself as the best brand, it must always steer clear of any kind or boardroom wrangles and court cases. If there are misunderstandings between managers or members of the board of a company, they should be solved privately and in a timely manner.

- Never associate your business with questionable individuals or companies

If you're thinking of registering a company, you must never do business or associate your company with questionable individuals and companies such as those being investigated by the IRS for tax evasion, money laundering, financing terrorism or illegal gangs and drug/human trafficking. You must also avoid doing business with companies suspected of safety violations that endanger the lives of employees or neighboring community. Qualified and experienced workers will avoid working for you if you are doing business with such companies.

- Avoid illegal dealings

Doing illegal businesses or closing underhand deals will bring down your company/business sooner than you think. Just think of what is going to happen once your illegal businesses or underhand deals are unraveled by the government. You could be prosecuted, your license can be suspended indefinitely or assets confiscated. Remember that such court cases are always lengthy and you might need to spend so much money on attorneys to defend you in court. If you're found guilty, you can be fined heavily or even imprisoned for several months or years. Consumers also tend to avoid companies and businesses involved in illegal activities and hence your brand will never grow once you start doing illegal businesses.

Effective Marketing Strategies

Incorporating a company/business is the easier part and the hard part is making sure that potential clients know the kind of services and/or products you are offering. Marketing also entails informing clients where they can find your products/services and the fees you'll be charging them. This means that small and newly established companies must always be on the lookout so as to identify opportunities to advertise their products/services. Before a potential client agrees to try out your services and/or products you must be able to convince them why they should believe you and not your competitors.

Here are some of the most effective marketing strategies that have been proven to work worldwide in any industry:

- Radio, television and print media advertisements

Believe it or not, even though radio, television and print media advertisements started decades ago, they are still some of the most effective methods of marketing products and therefore increasing customer numbers. There are more than a hundred million radios and televisions in the United States alone. Each day, millions of people watch TV or listen to their favorite radio stations. By simply advertising your business during prime times, you are guaranteed of growth in customer numbers and hence sales. When planning to place advertisements on radios and televisions it is important that you advertise during live events with the maximum anticipated audience. Some multinational companies are known to spend millions of dollars on a few seconds advertisement during popular events such as final NFL and NBA matches. Since millions of newspaper copies are sold in the United States each day, you can also advertise your products/services there so as to attract as many people as possible.

- Placing adverts on social media

Currently there are more than one billion active Facebook users worldwide. Other popular social websites such as Twitter, linked in and Whatsapp also have hundreds of millions of members. By simply placing advertisements in such websites you are guaranteed of significantly increasing your clientele and hence profits.

- Establishing an active website and blog

You can also market your business by creating a website with frequent updates on news related to your industry. The website must have accurate and detailed information about the products or services you are offering. This way a potential customer will know where to go if they want some clarification or want to find out more about the products/services. An active blog provides your customers a platform where they can share their experiences and get in touch with other customers. You can also advertise your products/services in other websites offering services/products related to yours and then backlink the advert to a page in your website.

- Sponsoring famous/renowned national or seasonal events

National and seasonal events such as professional bull riding competitions, theatrical performances, football matches, ballet performances, music festivals and high school games provide a platform for companies and businesses to advertise their merchandise to hundreds of thousands of people. By sponsoring a team participating in such events, you can grow a small business into a multimillion dollar empire with an expansive clientele. If you are not sponsoring any of the teams participating in these events, you can still advertise your products/services in or around venues where the events are held.

- Acquiring naming rights to widely visited venues/spots

There are more than two hundred arenas, amphitheaters and stadiums distributed across the United States. Sample a few of these venues and you'll discover that most of them are named after renowned businesses and companies. Acquiring the naming rights to highly visited venues is one of the best ways of advertising your company as you'll get a lot of exposure once an event is held there.

- Giving out incentives to customers

Another effective marketing strategy entails giving out incentives to customers as it helps nurture numerous loyal customers who are willing to buy your products/services at all costs. Such incentives include discounts on multiple purchases, free delivery of purchased commodities and providing warranty for electronic gadgets.

- Door to door campaigns and direct mails

Door to door campaigns and direct mails helps businesses sign in consumers who are not exposed to other forms of advertisements such as television, social media or newspapers. You can therefore boost your customer campaigns by marketing your products through direct mails or from door to door.

- Seasonal campaigns

Have you ever noticed that you will find Christmas trees and related products around mid-December? Well, you can increase your sales by taking advantage of such seasons to market your company. Keep in mind that such seasons are associated with gifts to friends and family. You can therefore encourage consumers to purchase your products as gifts for their loved ones during such seasons.

How to Penetrate a Highly Competitive Market

During the industrial revolution up to around the Second World War there was very little competition as there were very few industries and a limited variety of products on offer. However, currently there are countless number of companies and firms dealing in all types of businesses. This means that you must be prepared to encounter stiff competition regardless of the type of business you are planning to register.

You can easily penetrate a highly competitive market by implementing some of the tips listed below:

- Market analysis

Different people in different geographical or political regions have different preferences in particular products. You can penetrate a highly competitive environment by analyzing the market so as to establish what the local communities like and hate. This way you can be able to offer them what other companies can't. You can also analyze a given market so as to establish the most effective technique of advertising there.

- Invest in collecting information about competitors –intelligence

If you are thinking of penetrating a given market, you should invest some money in collecting information about what other companies are doing or planning to do. This way you can come up with counter measures to make sure that your customer numbers is not affected by your competitors' moves.

- Run a business based on quality and high number of sales instead of high profits

When establishing your business in a highly competitive market, you can reduce the price of your products so as to attract more customers. Whereas the profit made in each unit sold is reduced, the total profits will not be significantly affected as the number of sold units will increase. Whenever implementing this strategy, you must always make sure that the quality of products is not affected as a result of the increase in the number of sales.

- Get rid of all barriers between the company management and potential clients

Sometimes customers feel very disappointed if it takes an abnormally long period of time to receive purchased products or services. Your customer base will also remain stagnant if you never address all the raised issues or take a very long period of time to address them. If you are interested in penetrating a market with high competition, you must ensure that all the barriers between the company and potential clients are removed.

- Persistence and strategic advertisements

Even when sales remain constant after several weeks of advertisement, you shouldn't give up or pull out of the market all together. In the long run, more and more people will start getting used to your products and start purchasing them as their first choice. Strategic advertisement means placing adverts such that as many people as possible see them. For instance, you can schedule your adverts to be aired in all local TV or radio stations at the same time. This way, everybody watching a TV at that particular time will see the advert.

- Periodic analysis of your performance and improving on your shortcomings

After running advertisements for several months, you can hire a professional research firm so as to establish which adverts were most effective in a given state, area or for a given age group. Research should also be done so as to establish what wasn't appealing about your adverts or products. Once you have this information you can improve on your shortcomings while at the same time enhancing your positive side.

Survival Tactics during Harsh Economic Times and Dwindling Sales

All businesses have or will be affected by harsh economic conditions at some point in their existence. During conditions such as a recession or when the supply is excessively higher than the demand, the number of units sold reduces by a huge margin as most customers are trying to save as much money as possible. How you run a business during harsh economic conditions is what determines whether the business will survive or collapse. Entrepreneurs must always be alert and always on the lookout so as to adopt different strategies meant to counter these conditions.

Some of the best ways of surviving during unfavorable market conditions include the following:

- Cutting down on unnecessary expenditure

By cutting down on unnecessary expenditure, you can help your company stay afloat during harsh economic conditions as it helps boost the profits. During unfavorable conditions it is not necessary to spend company resources on things such as new office furniture when the existing one is in good condition. It is also not necessary to replace damaged electronic gadgets while they can be repaired at much cheaper costs.

- Insurance cover

Most insurance companies are willing to provide cover for all types of businesses. You can therefore cover your business against dwindling sales, litigations or accidents.

- Rebranding

Rebranding or re-launching a company can also boost a company's sales during difficult times because customers will feel like you are offering something new. You can also shake up the company's management so as to increase consumer confidence in your ability to offer them what they want. When rebranding or shaking up the company's management, you can split the business into different interdependent but independent units i.e. production, marketing, accounting, human resource, intelligence and planning. This way each unit will perform optimally as it will be easy to establish where there is a problem. You will easily know if one of the departments is underperforming and hence replace it with more qualified and experienced staff.

- Offering products/services on loan

You can also decide to offer products/services on loan as a way of ensuring that your customer numbers remains the same even during unfavorable market conditions. When offering products on loan, it is important that you ensure that the consumers are in a position to repay the money. If you fail to establish the consumers' ability to repay the loan, you can find yourself in an even bigger mess than the unfavorable market conditions.

Conclusion

You are on your way to becoming one of the most successful entrepreneurs by simply implementing the tips discussed in this book. When starting a business, it is important to note that not all the tips are applicable in all types of business/companies. You should therefore carefully analyze them before implementing those that are applicable in your specific business.

Different markets also respond differently to given products and hence it is up to you to do some research on what tactic will work in a given environment. However the ideas listed in this book will help you transform a small business into a multimillion dollar enterprise in an average market under normal conditions.

Remember that your level of preparedness and contingency plans is what will determine whether your business is going to be successful or be another example of failed investments. After reading the book "How to Transform a Small Business into a Multimillion Dollar Enterprise" you are now fully prepared to register any type of business, anywhere and start making profits.

Don't just sit and do nothing while other businessmen and women are transforming their companies, start implementing the ideas listed in this book and you'll be surprised at how fast your company will grow!!!

Author Bio

Colvin Tonya Nyakundi

Colvin Tonya Nyakundi is a professional freelance writer and co-author of 'How to Transform a Small Business into a Multimillion Dollar Enterprise.' Apart from that book, he has a portfolio of several other publications accumulated in the more than two years that he has been freelancing through www.odesk.com.

In addition to his interest in investment publications he has authored several personal relationships, survival, travel and holiday guides, and real estate publications. Other books that he has co-authored include 'How to Improve Your Communication Skills,' 'Construction Guide for New Investors in Real Estate,' 'How to Identify the Perfect Holiday Destination' and How to Prepare and Survive in a Foreign Country.' You can get in touch with him through his official Facebook account, tonyanc@facebook.com.

Check out some of the other JD-Biz Publishing books

Gardening Series on Amazon

Health Learning Series

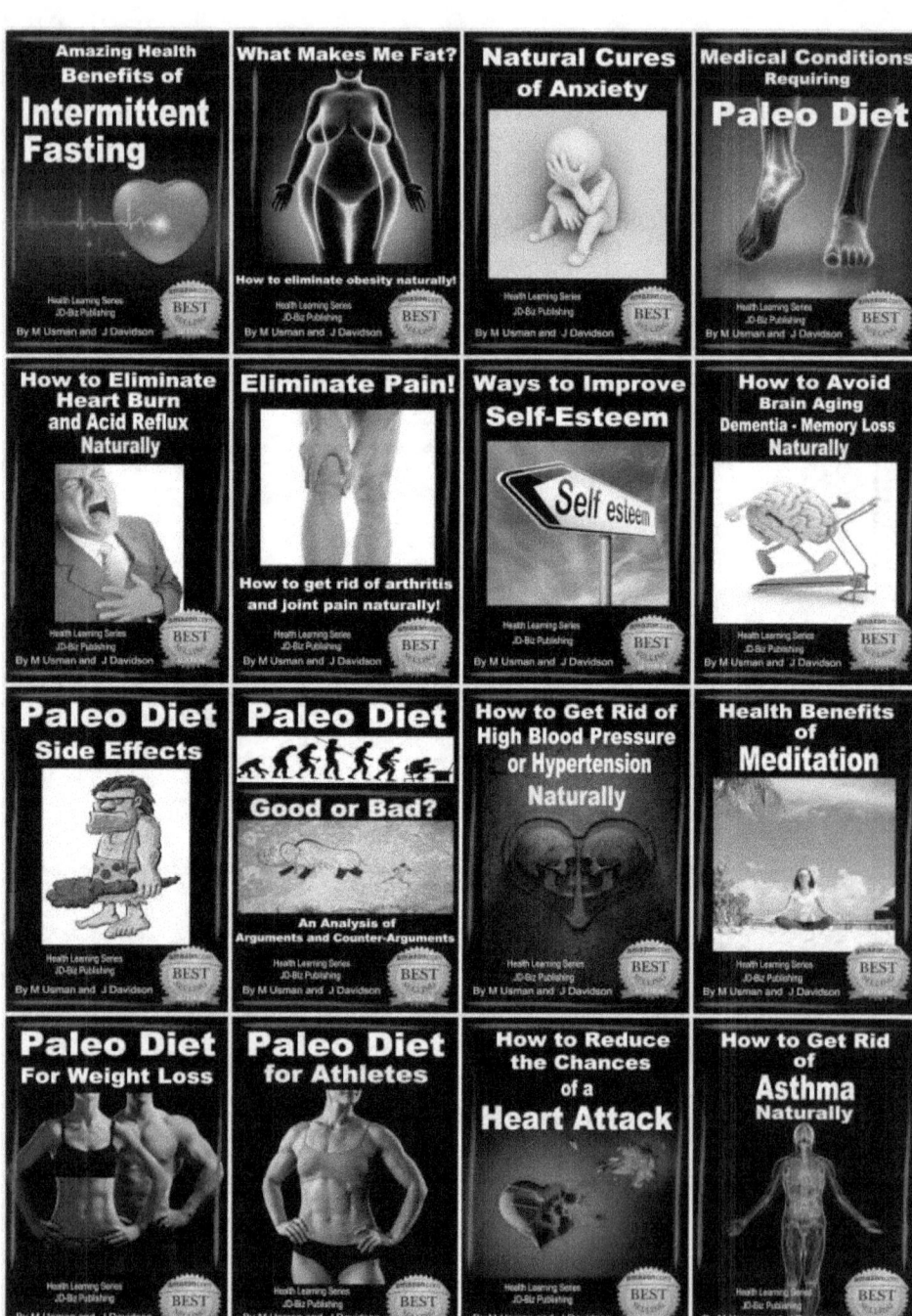

Learn To Draw Series

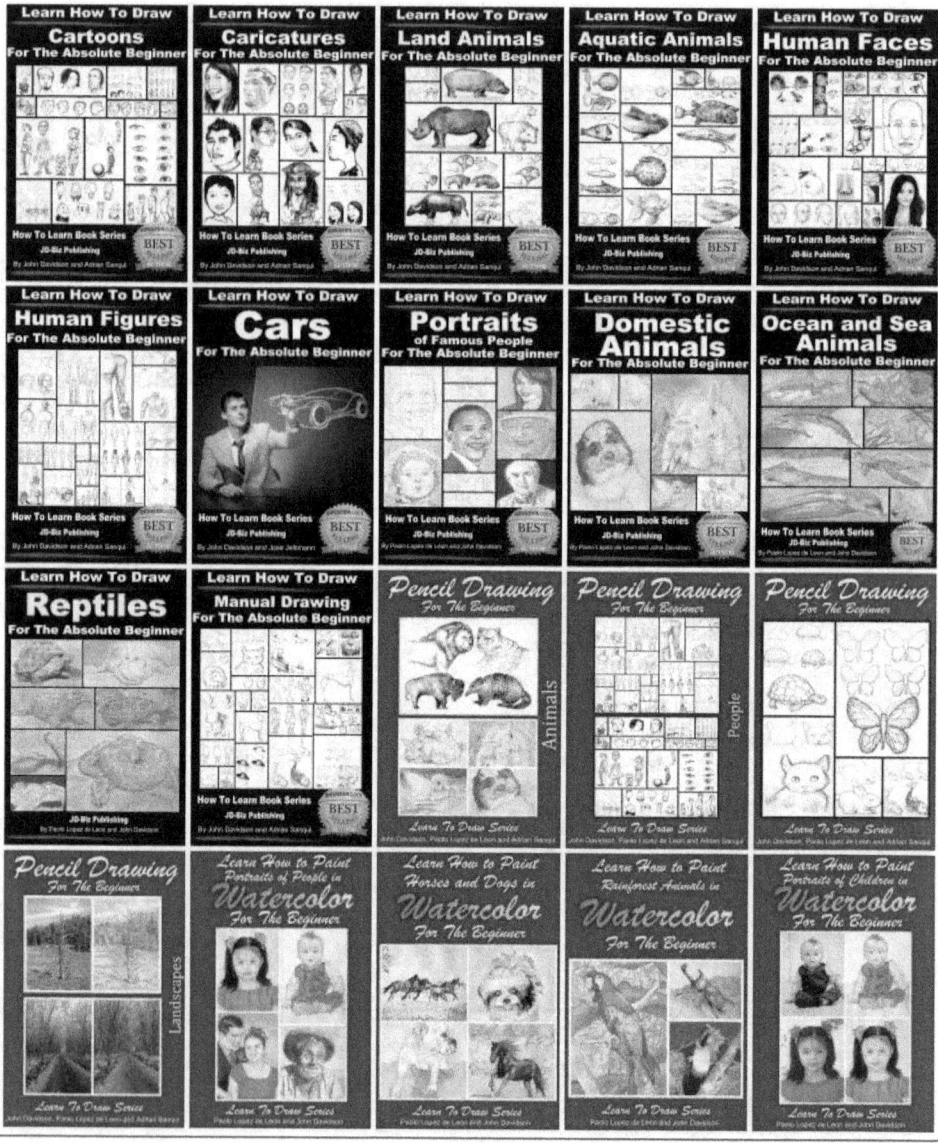

How to Build and Plan Books

Entrepreneur Book Series

Our books are available at

1. Amazon.com

2. Barnes and Noble

3. Itunes

4. Kobo

5. Smashwords

6. Google Play Books

Publisher

JD-Biz Corp

P O Box 374

Mendon, Utah 84325

http://www.jd-biz.com/

Mendon Cottage Books

P O Box 374, Mendon Utah 84325